IMAGES
of America

HAMTRAMCK
THE WORLD WAR II YEARS

On the cover: Jennie Kedzierski, a teacher at Pilsudski School, enlists the aid of students Bruno Ziomek, 11, and Mike Borushko, 13, to spread the message: "Remove labels, wash, cut out ends and flatten." Those were the instructions given as residents gathered tin cans for recycling in October 1943. (Hamtramck Historical Commission.)

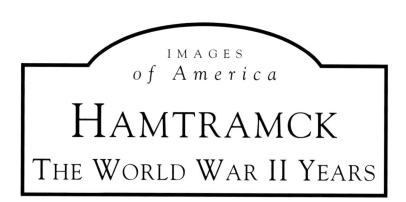

IMAGES
of America

HAMTRAMCK
THE WORLD WAR II YEARS

Greg Kowalski

ARCADIA
PUBLISHING

Published by Arcadia Publishing
Charleston SC, Chicago IL, Portsmouth NH, San Francisco CA

Printed in the United States of America

Library of Congress Catalog Card Number: 2007920805

For all general information contact Arcadia Publishing at:
Telephone 843-853-2070
Fax 843-853-0044
E-mail sales@arcadiapublishing.com
For customer service and orders:
Toll-Free 1-888-313-2665

Visit us on the Internet at www.arcadiapublishing.com

*This book is dedicated to my father, Joseph Kowalski Sr.,
who served in World War II, and to my mother,
Martha Violet Kowalski, who served at home.*

CONTENTS

ACKNOWLEDGMENTS

Almost all the photographs in the book came from the archives of the Hamtramck Historical Commission. The original source for many was the Hamtramck *Citizen* newspaper.

INTRODUCTION

From the early morning of September 1, 1939, to the evening of August 14, 1945, Hamtramckans took World War II personally.

This was not the case for all America, for the United States did not enter World War II until December 8, 1941. But for most of the people of Hamtramck, the war began when the army of Adolf Hitler crossed the border and invaded Poland two years before the Japanese attack on Pearl Harbor. The reaction in Hamtramck was an expression of horror, fear, and outrage.

In 1939, Hamtramck had a population of about 47,000 people, and more than 80 percent were Polish or of Polish descent. Many Hamtramckans had close relatives in Poland and they were personally touched by the tragedy in Europe.

Here Hitler was hanged in effigy—twice. Young men rushed to join the Polish army, but because the United States was not yet at war, the would-be volunteers were turned away or directed to the American army. In fact, Mayor Walter Kanar urged residents that they "must not become involved in this terrible catastrophe . . . our homes, our families and our lives are rooted here in American soil and here we must remain."

But he added, "We cannot close our minds and conscience. The citizens of Hamtramck are predominantly of Polish descent. Those who are not also sympathize with the victims of any aggression. We can, without contravening or transgressing against any of the restrictions placed upon a true neutral, express that sympathy toward Poland, the land of our forefathers."

Within days, fund-raising for Poland began and a substantial amount of money was collected. In the space of two days following the start of the war, $6,294 was collected for Poland at Edmund Krotkiewicz's delicatessen. The scene was repeated at places all over the city.

With the bombing of Pearl Harbor on December 7, 1941, the United States was fully committed to the war. In Hamtramck, the transition to being at war brought a variety of changes. Within five days of the declaration of the war, a municipal defense council was formed and preparations were made to defend against an air attack. A call went out for volunteers to serve as air raid wardens and soon the men with the white metal helmets and "CD" arm bands became a common sight as they patrolled the streets during blackouts, looking for light leaking from curtained windows.

Sales of war bonds doubled in the space of one week and young men rushed to join the U.S. Army, U.S. Navy, U.S. Marines, and Coast Guard. Women enlisted in the Women's Air Corps and WAVES (Women Appointed for Voluntary Emergency Service). Still the area selective service office was instructed to do business as usual. The December 1941 quota of draftees was not changed after the attack on Pearl Harbor. But there was no doubt that we were in for a fight.

As the *Citizen* newspaper of December 12, 1941, wrote on the front page: "We're really in a war to the death. It's safe to say that the bombing of our Pacific territories is only the beginning of a titanic struggle. Never before in the history of our nation has our very existence been threatened as seriously as it is today." The assessment was accurate.

Marine corporal John Targosz of Moran Street was the first from Hamtramck to die. He was killed on September 12, 1942, in the Solomon Islands. Many more would follow. Nearly 200 Hamtramckans were killed in World War II, and long after the war, bodies were still being returned from far away places.

On the home front, life changed quickly and dramatically. Industries, particularly the massive Hamtramck Assembly Plant, commonly known as the Dodge Main plant, turned to war production. The workforce changed as well. More women were getting jobs in the factories as the men went into the service. Families were split up as husbands, sons, and brothers were sent to military bases across the country and then overseas.

Some new fathers did not see their children for years and then for only brief periods while they were on leave. Basic commodities were suddenly in short supply. Sugar, meat, coffee, flour, gasoline, tires, and other items were rationed. Trash became valuable. Kids collected paper, foil, metal, even junk cars to be recycled for the war effort.

Of course, not everyone in Hamtramck was of Polish descent and the hardships imposed by the war were spread among all. African Americans, Ukrainians, Russians, and other ethnic groups made their contribution to the war effort, serving in the military and carrying on as best as anyone could at home.

It was not easy. With shortages being so persistent, building projects had to be put off, and you could forget about buying a new car. The factories were producing Jeeps, not jalopies. More than anything the sense of the war hung over everything. America's involvement in World War II lasted less than four years, but it dominated almost every aspect of life.

Families were broken apart for years and there was the constant threat that the dreaded telegram would arrive announcing the death of a loved one. Yet for the most part, life went on as usual. Bickering, which was a hallmark of Hamtramck's politics from the day it incorporated as a city, continued unabated. But the administration of Mayor Stephen Skrzycki, elected to office in 1942, ushered in a new era of political stability and clean government. Hamtramck began to lose its image as a wide-open city that reveled in flaunting Prohibition as it became known as a key supplier in the arsenal of democracy.

As it had from the day it produced its first car in 1914, the Dodge Main automobile plant dominated Hamtramck, only instead of producing Dodges and Plymouths it was building war vehicles.

Hamtramck played a direct role in bringing the war to an end, as well. Emil Konopinski, a graduate of Hamtramck High School, was one of the five key scientists who developed the atomic bomb.

The end of the war was welcomed in Hamtramck like it was across the world, and it had a profound effect on the city. The soldiers returned home, and armed with the GI Bill, which provided low-interest, zero down payment home loans, many Hamtramckans left the city for the suburbs.

But Hamtramck endured the loss of population just as it withstood the privations of war. And while the city has changed much in the wake of World War II, the people never forgot the sacrifices made by so many to preserve the way of life we have today.

One

ON THE BRINK

Like all of America, Hamtramck was struggling to emerge from the Great Depression in the late 1930s. The economy was recovering somewhat from the Great Depression, and New Deal projects funded by federal government programs, like the Works Progress Administration, brought some improvements to the city in the form of a new post office and sports stadium as well as providing jobs. In 1938 alone, some 1,500 men were hired to pave and widen streets and alleys across town.

But life was still precarious. And there were clouds of war forming on the horizon. Adolf Hitler was on the march across Europe and it was clear that Poland was a target. That was a cause for grave concern, but little could be done.

Life went on. Kids and their parents enjoyed playing in the big wading pool at Conant Street and Holbrook Street. They also would go to movies at the Farnum, Martha Washington, and Conant Theaters, or one of the other four movies houses operating in town to see Jane Withers in *Boy Friend*, or Richard Dix in *Man of Conquest*, or J. Farrell MacDonald in *The Last Alarm*. Adults might stop by the Bowery night club and catch a major entertainer like Danny Thomas or Sophie Tucker. Dances were frequently held and records were plentiful at the local stores. And there was high school football. The big game between Detroit Catholic Central and Hamtramck High School in November 1939 drew 11,402 paying fans to see the game at Keyworth Stadium. Alas, Hamtramck lost, 20-0.

After Hitler's army invaded Poland on September 1, 1939, the sense of the state of war grew. In October 1940, that was strengthened when the draft was instituted. In all, 8,250 Hamtramck men registered for the first draft. Many more would follow.

They knew what to expect. In December 1939, there were 2,500 people jammed into Copernicus Junior High School to hear Eustazy Borkowski, captain of the Polish steamship *Batory*, relate his early war experiences. The following month, Polish army general Joseph Haller was greeted by thousands when he visited Hamtramck with the message that Poland would rise again.

Europe was ablaze in November 1940, but the United States was not yet at war. And while relatives fretted abut relations in the line of fire, there still were light moments at home. Jimmy Durante (center) generated smiles when he visited the American Legion Henry Bushway Post 14. With him, from left to right are Walter Kraft; Frank Barbaro, owner of the Bowery night club where Durante often performed; Frank Leach; and William Ratajack.

With the war just weeks away, defense bonds were being sold in November 1941. Taking part in a bond promotion from left to right are Edward Kopeck, Irene Tompor, Ann O'Hara, Martha Andrachik, and Bernard Harris.

The "Defense of Democracy" was the theme of a banner being carried in a parade down Jos. Campau Street in 1941. By then it was clear that the war was likely to engulf the United States. But where and when? (Joseph Lucas collection.)

An Armistice Day parade down Jos. Campau Street in November 1937 was especially poignant as Adolf Hitler was making demands for parts of Europe. Note the streetcar lines down the center of the street and the Campau Theater at left, one of seven neighborhood theaters that were the chief venues of entertainment in the 1940s.

On the eve of World War II, Hamtramck was a bustling place, and Jos. Campau Street was its main artery. Dave Stober's clothing store was one of the most popular shops in town and became a landmark for years. (Joseph Lucas collection.)

Hamtramckans already were fighting a war in early December 1941 when the city took up arms against the rat population. Hamtramck Department of Public Works superintendent Fred Pabst oversees Jack Pachesnik as he inserts a gas hose into a rat hole in the side of a building. Carbon dioxide would be pumped into the hole, killing or flushing out the rats.

War clouds notwithstanding, taxes are inevitable. Former city councilman Stanley Sporny was hit with a city tax totaling a whopping $1.92 in 1939.

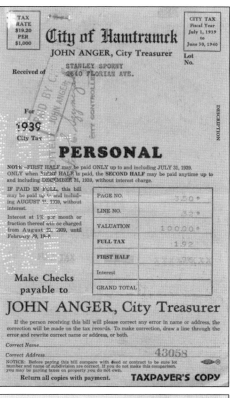

The Lone Ranger, Joe E. Brown, and Dick Powell provided a diversion from the struggle of the lingering Great Depression in the late 1930s. Farnum Theatre was one of the major movie houses in town offering a constantly changing bill of fare.

Boxing champ Jack Dempsey (right) visited with Mayor Walter Kanar in 1940. Kanar was known to toss a few potent punches himself.

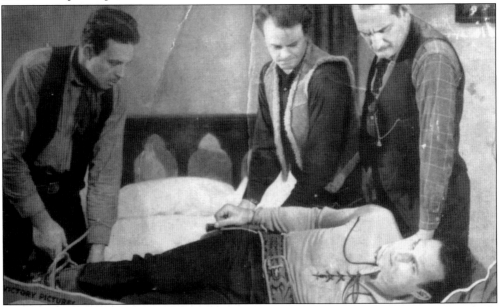

Tom Tyler (laying down) made dozens of Westerns in the 1930s and 1940s. Originally a body builder who lived in Hamtramck and worked at the Hamtramck Assembly Plant (more commonly known as the Dodge Main plant), he was noticed by a Hollywood scout who spotted him at a body building competition. Tyler's acting range was limited but he was exceptionally successful. Along with acting in numerous "B" Westerns, like *Cheyenne Rides Again*, he appeared in such classics as John Ford's *Stagecoach* in 1939. He also was Captain Marvel in the movie serials and even did a stint as the Mummy in *The Mummy's Hand*. By the early 1940s, he was the number one Western star in America.

Bluebird and Victor records were popular at Naimark Company on Jos. Campau Street. Florence Naimark shows a customer what is new in November 1941. Naimark boasted a large record department, including Polish tunes.

Corinthian Missionary Baptist Church was founded in 1917 and grew through the years. By the early 1940s, the congregation was able to move to a new building on Caniff Street and is shown as the members paraded to the new building. Parishioners from the church also saw service in the war. Corinthian Baptist now occupies a new building near the old church.

The ZT Super Market at Joseph Campau and Lehman Streets was typical of the many small markets operating throughout the city. Owner Z. Tomaszewski offered poultry, meats, fresh fruits, vegetables, and canned goods. The store is pictured in October 1941, just before the start of the war.

The Works Progress Administration (WPA) sponsored a broad range of projects, including providing jobs for artists. Between 1937 and 1941, local artists were hired to paint a series of pictures such as this one, depicting a typical post office of the day. More than 60 such paintings were done for the Hamtramck Public School District and were displayed in school buildings. After missing for decades, they turned up in a Grosse Pointe Park art gallery in 2001. The WPA was disbanded shortly after the war began as nearly everyone involved was drafted or found work in war industries.

Hamtramckan Joseph Solo stands beside one of his trucks. Solo got involved in the trucking industry at age 11, and by age 21 he owned 17 trucks and ran his own company paving, crushing concrete, and excavating. Perhaps his biggest job was as a lead contractor on the construction of the Davison Freeway in 1941–1942.

Solo's trucks are shown at work on the Davison Freeway. The Davison Freeway was started before the war began and was finished in 1942. It was the first freeway in the United States and would open a new chapter in transportation. The freeway would play a critical role in connecting the metro area with the growing number of war manufacturing plants on the west side.

In the years of the Great Depression of the 1930s, Hamtramck still managed to conduct some major construction projects—thanks mainly to the federal government's WPA program. The government allotted about $185,000 for the construction of Keyworth Stadium in 1936. The city pitched in with $45,000 of its own. Across town, the city also built a new post office through the WPA.

Keyworth Stadium was still a new facility as the war approached. It immediately became a focal point of the city where foreign dignitaries spoke during visits to town and Hamtramck High School graduation ceremonies were held. Bands played and more than a few football games were battled there.

Jos. Campau Street, across from the giant Dodge Main factory, was a cluttered but busy string of businesses in the late 1930s and early 1940s. They catered to the thousands of workers at the giant factory. Soon they would serve the factory in another way—be being demolished to make way for a pedestrian overpass over the congested street.

Just days before the attack on Pearl Harbor, city clerk Albert Zak notched a victory of his own. He bagged a 175-pound buck on a hunting trip up north. Naturally, Hamtramck politics being what they were, reports were circulated that Zak had actually bought the beast.

There was nothing subtle about Leo Rau's approach to business or advertising. Rau operated the popular House of Rau bar on Jos. Campau Street. It was noted for the incredible collection of, well, junk suspended from the ceiling. Rau also dabbled, unsuccessfully, in politics. This postcard noted his new address.

Members of the Hamtramck Municipal Bowling League gather for a photograph just before the start of the war. Soon the war would overshadow such carefree fun.

Two

A City at War

Just like that, America was at war. But what did that mean?

There was no enemy in sight and the attack on Pearl Harbor occurred half a world away. A front page article in the *Citizen* summed up the mood three days before Christmas in 1941, "There'll be as much Christmas festivities in Hamtramck and North Detroit this year as ever, even though war clouds appeared over the holiday horizon for the first time in 23 years."

Crowds jammed every store in Hamtramck during the week as Christmas shoppers were out in full force. Yet there was an appreciation of the situation. Within five days of the start of the war, a call went out for volunteers to serve on the newly formed civilian defense council. The perception of an actual attack on the city was real. It was thought that German bombers could fly across the Atlantic using Greenland as a stopover point. Dodge Main would make a tempting target. That led to staging of periodic blackouts and air-raid drills.

The plant was in line for some major changes as it shifted over to production of war material. The workforce would change too, with women moving in to fill the jobs vacated by the men who were drafted into the service. Rationing was instituted and common-place items, like sugar and gasoline, became scarce commodities. Save, reuse, devote everything possible to the war effort was the message stressed repeatedly. Scrap even was sold to finance the purchase of a tank in the name of Hamtramck. The citizens were infused with a sense of patriotism and appreciation of the seriousness of the situation. That was partly manifested in the seemingly endless war bond and stamp sales. Everyone was urged to buy bonds individually or as part of groups to help finance the war. Even the local theaters sold bonds.

The war quickly became everyone's battle for survival.

The Civilian Defense Control Center was set up to coordinate response efforts in case the city was bombed. Needed services, such as ambulances, gas officers, and even decontamination officers could be dispatched to attack sites. The system was tested in February 1943, with Stanley Miller (left) and Leo Latkowski manning the command panel.

Sgt. Bill Burns of Newton Street returned on leave in November 1943 with a tale to tell about battling the Japanese in New Guinea. While home he visited his prewar boss, Bill Harrison, who owned Harrison clothing store on East Davison Street. Burns made a point of telling the local newspaper that he was of Ukrainian descent.

In March 1943, a shipment of helmets and chemical fire extinguishers arrived to protect the city. The National Office of Civil Defense sent the city 1,512 steel helmets and 1,900 chemical gas tanks. In addition, the city received 1,567 gas masks, 120 cots, and additional firefighting equipment. Looking over the new material are, from left to right, Walter Nowosad, Frank Piasecki, and Michael Palczarski. Piasecki was the chief air raid warden.

Henry Dzialo, owner of Doc's Esquire Dar on Jos. Campau Street, displays a Japanese flag sent to him by Hamtramck Marines Cpl. Harry Mirek, Pfc. Stanley Borowiec, Pvt. Chester Karolski, and Pvt. Zigmund Bagnowski who had captured it at Guadalcanal in May 1943. The flag came with instructions to hang it in the bar "until you and your customers are tired of looking and swearing at it."

In recognition of reaching its wartime production goal, Advance Plating Company, on Klinger Street, was presented with an Army-Navy E Award pennant in January 1943. Taking part in the presentation from left to right are Col. August M. Krech, of the U.S. Army; Oliver Horsch, employee representative; Bernard Bauer, Advance president; and U.S. Navy commander S. J. Singer.

In July 1943, civil defense officers gathered at Veterans Memorial Park. Dozens of men volunteered for duty, patrolling the streets during blackouts to make sure that windows were light-sealed. They were ready to respond with aid if an attack should occur. None ever did. However, in June 1942, 15 persons were fined $10 to $20 and one man was sent to jail for five days for violating the blackout.

In March 1942, the lobby of the Martha Washington Theatre on Jos. Campau Street was turned into a voluntary draft registration center. While soldiers-to-be registered, the theater showed films on the selective service. Standing over the proceedings is theater manager Frank Strukel. Seated, from left to right, are Fritz Rykowski, Jane Nowakowski, and Rose Mankowski.

Small but powerful, Lt. Ludmilla Pavliczenko was an extraordinary sniper, credited with killing 309 Nazis. But she was a demure lady as she visited Hamtramck City Hall in October 1943. Greeting her are city clerk Albert Zak, Mrs. Cass Cooper, Sgt. Cass Cooper, city union president Chester Reese, councilman Frank Sosnowski, and council president Walter Serement.

Bud Abbott (left) and Lou Costello (third from left) were two of the biggest stars in Hollywood when they made a special appearance at Veterans Memorial Park in August 1942 for a bond rally. As part of the festivities, the comic duo was presented with police night sticks by Bob Hall. In the background, second from left, is Morris Direnfeld of the Krohngold Shoes store.

Mugging for the camera, Abbott and Costello snuggle up with Ethel Shepherd, a singer at the popular Club Stevadora in Detroit. Bending over the three is Joe Kargol, editor of the *Citizen* newspaper.

Abbott takes the microphone with a hand from Costello. About 4,000 people attended the bond rally and wildly greeted the duo as they arrived on a fire truck at Veterans Memorial Park in August 1942. The event was an incredible success, as some $250,000 in war bonds was raised in the three days preceding their appearance on a Monday night. At one point in the rally they generated $85,000 in pledges in the space of a few minutes. In the background are Bob Hall (left), master of ceremonies for the event, and *Citizen* newspaper editor Joseph Kargol, who was one of the chief organizers. The event was one of the highlights of the city's entire war effort.

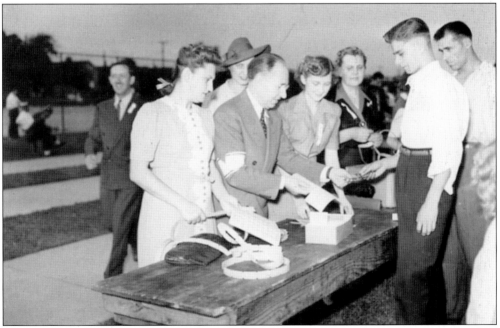

Max Rosenbaum of Max's Jewelry pitched in, serving at one of the tables where war stamps were sold at the Abbott and Costello bond rally. The stamps were brought in by armored trucks and sold by the thousands.

"Who will buy a bond?" Lou Costello asked the crowd at the bond rally. Thousands responded. "I love you all," Costello told the crowd of 4,000 attending. He said that we must do "everything possible to beat the murderer who is loose in Europe . . . Unless we beat him, we are liable to lose our families, our lives, our happiness, our freedom and our property."

Mayor Stephen Skrzycki (right) conducted his own war bond drive and made a big sale in April 1943 when Alex Krot contributed $10,000. The Krot Funeral Home is a longtime Hamtramck business, and Krot opened his own funeral home on Van Dyke in Detroit by this time.

Col. Paul V. Engstrom, assistant state director of selective service and Wayne County director of selective service, spoke to the Hamtramck Rotary Club in November 1942 to discuss its operations and its flexible rules regarding deferments due to family and jobs. With him from left to right are Joseph Mitchell, chairman of one of the two selective service boards in the city; John Amos, secretary of the Rotary Club; and Edmund Krotkiewicz, chairman of the city's second selective service board.

Youngsters also were involved in the effort as part of the Civilian Air Patrol (CAP), which included a girls unit. Malina Kotowski, 19, a member of the girls unit, goes over CAP plans at Hamtramck High School with Lt. Ralph Berkhausen, the intelligence officer in charge of the Hamtramck unit in March 1944. With them are, from left to right, Sgt. Don Kay, school trustee Edward Kopek, city council president Walter Serement, and Sgt. Henry Selasky, the squadron clerk.

Keys were made of brass and brass was a vital war commodity. In August 1942, the Hamtramck Junior Red Cross began a drive to collect old keys. Julia Pezda Antonowicz displays a copy of a poster that was placed at stores, churches, and municipal buildings.

Kids collected scrap, which was piled up at the local schools. This impressive collection, gathered at the St. Ladislaus School playground in November 1942, even included an old car. Not to be outdone, the kids at cross-town rival St. Florian (below) collected their own mound of scrap—including another car.

Common council president Walter Serement presents a St. Christopher medal to Col. Jan Jankowski, who was in charge of the Polish Air Force training in Canada. Jankowski and a dozen Polish officers visited the common council in June 1942, just before they were to leave for England. The St. Christopher medal was a treasured possession of Serement, who wanted the officers to have it. St. Christopher is the patron saint of travelers.

Showing true patriotic spirit Cpl. Chester Kolodziejski (left) buys $700 worth of war bonds from Frank Strukel, manager of the Martha Washington Theatre in October 1943. Kolodziejski saved the money from his army pay. Watching the transaction is Kolodziejski's 2-year-old nephew Zig Stasz Jr.

Early into the war effort, buying war bonds was the patriotic thing to do. In January 1942, members of the Italian Club of Hamtramck did their part. Looking over a bond package are club members, from left to right, Peter Manzoni, Jimmy Simeone, and William Fraze.

Even members of the draft board were subject to the draft—for the most part. E. G. Van DeVenter, at age 73, was exempt. But fellow board members Edmund Krotkiewicz, age 45, and Robert Dickinson, age 61, did have to register as men ages 45 to 65 had to in May 1942. On Monday, April 27, 1942, about 6,200 Hamtramck men registered for the draft.

Dolls, toy planes, and Santa captured the attention of children at the Tau Beta Community House just a few weeks after the attack on Pearl Harbor. None had any idea of what the future held. Don McColl served as Santa for, from left to right, Theodore DeJutis, Mary Szenski, and Louise Riemann.

Even before the start of the war, poppies were sold to aid disabled veterans. But the collection took on an added significance by May 1942 when America was deep into the conflict. Mayor Stephen Skrzycki helped the cause, buying a poppy from Rose Claire Osiowiz, age 7. The sale was conducted by the American Legion and Polish Legion of American Veterans.

"Buy war bonds." The message was hammered over and over. Florian Manteuffel (left), manager of the Martha Washington Theatre, shares some bonds with Arthur Slepski in October 1942.

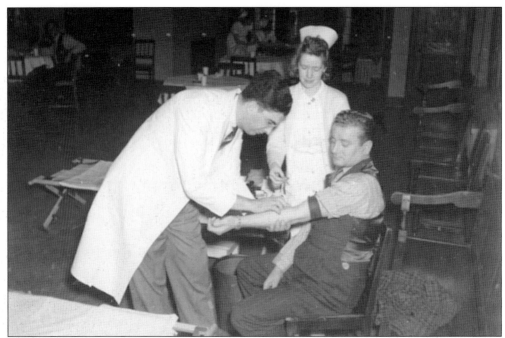

Chester Reese, president of the city employees' union, prepares to donate blood at the Tau Beta Community House in January 1942. Dr. L. E. Heideman, of the Red Cross, is assisted by nurse Phyllis Terry. On that day 60 men donated blood, which was used for wounded soldiers.

War, like politics, makes for strange alliances. In October 1942, Hamtramck mayor Stephen Skrzycki (second from left) participated in a program to welcome an unidentified visiting Russian hero. In other times the Russians and Poles would have stood apart as enemies.

Making plans for war, members of the Civilian Air Patrol and Office of Civil Defense determined how they would stage a realistic battle at Veterans Memorial Park on June 20, 1943. The big event drew 5,000 spectators who witnessed guns firing and the burning of buildings, set on fire to make the attack as realistic as possible. Making plans for the event from left to right are (first row) Capt. Sam Buck, of the CAP; Lt. Robert Saley, commanding officer of the Quartermaster Company at Fort Wayne; and Edward Kopek, event general chairman; (second row) Lt. Robert Lunceford, CAP commander, and Frank Piasecki, chief air raid warden.

With Swedish Crucible as a backdrop, the Hamtramck auxiliary police, the auxiliary firefighters, and the air raid wardens' team faced each other in a drill competition at Veterans Memorial Park as part of the big demonstration of how prepared they were to face an enemy attack.

To make the demonstration as realistic as possible, small buildings were erected at the park and set on fire. The civilian defense officers showed their skill in battling the blazes. There were real fears the city would be subjected to firebomb attacks.

The Hamtramck police triumphed as they won the trophy for having the best drill team in the office of civil defense competition with the air raid wardens and auxiliary firefighters. Hoisting the trophy are, from left to right, Col. Owen J. Cleary, who was an event judge; Edward Kopek, general chairman of the event; police sergeant John Kowalski, auxiliary police drill leader; and C. J. Maloney, head of the auxiliary police.

This bus is typical of the day. Cars were expensive and became scarce during the war years. Most people relied on the buses and streetcars for transportation. Although unimpressive, this vehicle proved to be the way of the future, at least as far a public transportation was concerned, as the buses replaced the streetcars entirely in the mid-1950s.

"One and all for victory," reads the sign carried by the kids of Our Lady Queen of Apostles School. Sister Octavia led the kids in a drive to collect scrap paper in March 1943.

The kids did a credible job collecting paper, as these youngsters show, perched atop a mountain of old newspapers collected in May 1944. The paper was stored in a basement room at the Our Lady Queen of Apostles School before being shipped off to a mill for recycling.

The kids recruited into the war effort helped ensure that nothing would go to waste. Those old tires that were annoying scrap in years before suddenly became resources to help defeat the enemy. Posing with a pile of "trash" that was being sorted to be reused in July 1942 are, from left to right, Alice Jaworski, Louise Danielowski, Chesterine Osustowicz, Arlene Pytkowski, Ronald Harasikiewiz, Sylvia Danielowski, and Stanley Blatt.

"Tighten your belt!" The message went out in Polish that sacrifices had to be made in this advertisement, which appeared in Polish in the *Citizen* newspaper. The full-page advertisement was sponsored by the popular Bowery night club.

A nattily dressed John Wojtylo, city councilman, hopped on a tractor in April 1944 to promote the planting of victory gardens. There was not much open space left in Hamtramck at that time, but residents were encouraged to make use of every bit of it. Hamtramck won several national awards for sponsoring victory gardens around town during the war years. The gardens not only offered a cheap source of food but also freed up resources that could be sent to troops overseas.

"Heads up, America, a land that is prepared can never die," so went the "Civil Defense March," a rousing tribute to America and reminder that people had to be ever-vigilant against the enemy threat.

Wounded solders at the Percy Jones General Hospital in Battle Creek benefited from 1,382 books and magazines collected by the Junior Commando units in May 1944. Examining the material are Steve Medvec, Frank Sparagowski, Phyllis and Sylvia Siennicki, and Martha Raczkowski.

Girl Scouts of Tau Beta Troop 171, led by Berta Engler, participated in making items like blankets for refugees, toys and scrap books for hospitals, and cookies for the USO in January 1944. With Engler are, from left to right, Marilyn Fralowicz, 11, Bernadine Vivnik, 11, and Frances Priess, 11.

Setting an example, Max's Jewelry Company presented $1,200 in war bonds and stamps to its employees in May 1942. Max Rosenbaum said it was his way of impressing the necessity of paying for the war and ultimately ensuring victory over world tyrants. At the presentation from left to right are Dr. M. A. Rosensweet, Rosenbaum, Wanda Poremski, Alfreda Jaracz, Helen Baranewicz, Claire Urbanik, Bernice Schmidt, and Charles Martin.

Mrs. Justine Horyszny checks out the $2,000 canteen truck donated to the city by Immaculate Conception Ukrainian Catholic Church in September 1942. The canteen was to be used by the Red Cross in case of emergencies. With her is city council president Walter Serement (left) and pastor Fr. Stephen Chehansky.

Father Chehanski and Serement examine the canteen truck donated by the Immaculate Conception Ukrainian Catholic Church parish. The vehicle was displayed at the parish's new church on Commor Street and old one on Grayling Street in September 1942.

With 6 million square feet of floor space, 30 miles of conveyors, 5,700 machines, and as many as 45,000 employees, Dodge Main was a powerful cog in the American war machine. Founded in 1910 by John and Horace Dodge, Dodge Main reached its peak operation during the war years. Both Dodge brothers died in 1920, within months of each other, and the factory eventually was sold to the Chrysler Corporation in the late 1920s.

Never a dull moment in HAMTRAMCK

No American city is closer to the battles than Hamtramck.

Its working citizens have made their mark upon the war. Its sons and daughters are in there fighting it.

Pictures coming home from invasion beaches and remote fields of action tell the story of Hamtramck—and of Dodge Dependability—as Allied ships, guns and fighting vehicles press home the attack.

Note — Hamtramck is a big and independent city entirely within the boundaries of Detroit. Dodge plants, laboratories and offices comprise some of its major institutions, employing more than 20,000 men and women in war production work.

For the better navigation and the greater safety of both fighting and cargo ships—Dodge makes the famous Sperry Gyro-Compass in quantity production.

Dodge makes Ambulances for the U.S. Army. They are vehicles of mercy on every battle front, companions and team-mates to the Dodge fighting trucks.

Dodge makes basic parts for the famous Bofors Anti-Aircraft Cannon, used for land and sea defense in almost every Allied field of action.

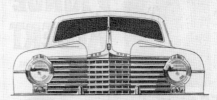

The millions of Dodge cars (and trucks) that give source and background to this enormous war production have, of course, been throttled down to the slower speeds and limited mileage of war-time. But their dependable qualities assert themselves, the world over, in this vital military form.

Dodge

DIVISION OF CHRYSLER CORPORATION

BACK THE ATTACK — WITH WAR BONDS

5

As one of the largest factories in the world, Dodge Main was seen as a potentially tempting target for German bombers. This large advertisement, which appeared in a national magazine, let the country know that Dodge Main was making a major contribution to the war effort.

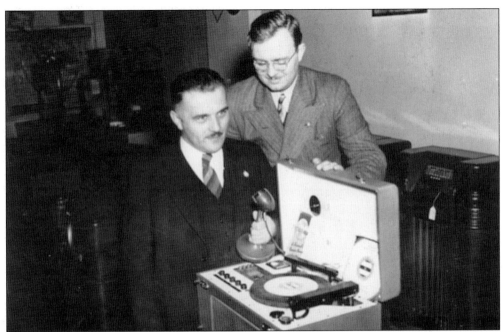

Sending a recorded message to a loved one in the service became a common practice by 1942. Judge Nicholas Gronkowski (left) records a message at Bejnar's Music House on Jos. Campau Street. Owner Henry Bejnar watches. The records were sent to the soldiers who could play the record at a USO quarters, record a message on the reverse side, and send it back.

Hamtramck tested its air raid control center in June 1942. Reviewing operations are the key members of the civil defense squad, from left to right, Fire Chief John Griffin; Charles Mariani, in charge of water mains; Anna Winkler, associate civilian defense coordinator; Frank Piasecki, chief air raid warden; Clarence Cole, commander of the Citizens Defense Corps in Hamtramck; Frank Kunkel, controller of the center; and police chief John Sikorski.

Hamtramck firefighters received 1,900 chemical tanks in March 1943 to fight incendiary bomb fires. Stanley Stecko is kneeling. Sanding, from left to right, are William Oldenburg, Frank Kowalczyk, Ed Oleksiak, and Carl Dobrzycki.

More than 130 prominent Polish Americans sent a desperate plea to Pres. Franklin D. Roosevelt in May 1942 "for justice for Poland." Underlying the theme of the 27-page document, in English and Polish, was that Poland must not be partitioned as it had been in the past and eventually be restored to its former borders as a free nation. Part of that was realized after the war when Poland was restored, but it would be decades before Poland would be free of Russian Communist control.

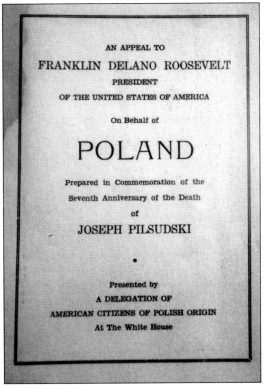

AN APPEAL TO

FRANKLIN DELANO ROOSEVELT

PRESIDENT

OF THE UNITED STATES OF AMERICA

On Behalf of

POLAND

Prepared in Commemoration of the
Seventh Anniversary of the Death

of

JOSEPH PILSUDSKI

•

Presented by

A DELEGATION OF

AMERICAN CITIZENS OF POLISH ORIGIN

At The White House

Pvt. Lou Stober was on a three-day leave when he stopped by to see his brother Dave at the store they operated together on Jos. Campau Street in December 1942. The Dave Stober clothing store was a Hamtramck landmark for decades. Lou was stationed at Camp Lee in Virginia.

For having more than 90 percent of the students participate in the war bond and stamp drive, the students at St. Ladislaus School were allowed to fly the Minute Man flag in June 1944. From left to right, Joseph Krzyzewski, Regina Kowalczyk, Melanie Zalenski, Norman Paluszewski, Fr. Alphonse Madeja, and Jean Bolewcki prepare to raise the flag in front of the school.

Candy is the order of the day with this donation to the Hamtramck Servicemen's Center in August 1943. Councilmen John Anger (left) and Frank Sosnowski donated the items to Helen Zubel (second from left), a WAVE, and Pfc. Mary Ann Krupa, of the Women's Army Corps (WAC).

As his best customers went off to war, Peter Ivanoff started placing their photographs on a wall of honor at his pool hall on Caniff Street. The display grew larger as the war dragged on.

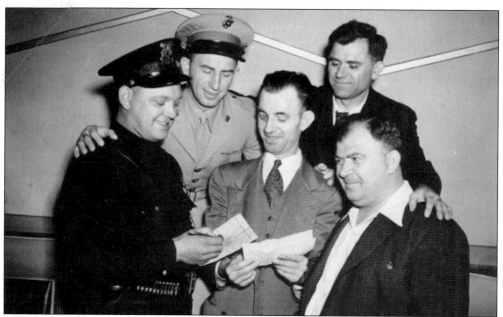

Bond sale efforts were paying off in September 1943, as police patrolman John Pietrzak and Marine second lieutenant Thaddeus Banachowski accept $3,000 in checks from Johnny Naidovich and Vasil Georgevich, owners of Three Star Bar-B-Q on Jos. Campau Street, and Stanley Wolski. The restaurant contributed $5,000 to the third bond sale. Pietrzak was the volunteer bond salesman for the police department.

Motorists had to display gasoline and mileage ration stickers to show they were conforming with the restrictions made necessary by the demands of the war.

The city teamed up with the American Red Cross in June 1943 to buy ambulances through the sale of war bonds. City clerk Albert Zak (left) and council president Walter Serement work with Motor Corps sergeant Albina Krecioch to arrange for the sale, which was to be conducted from a canteen truck parked on Jos. Campau Street.

To generate support for the forces in Europe, the Polish soldiers periodically would visit Hamtramck. Here, in June 1942, members of the Polish air force visit with city officials. They were treated as heroes.

Pondering the fate of the World War I cannon in Winfield Park in front of St. Francis Hospital are, from left to right, council president Walter Serement, Mayor Stephen Skrzycki, and Adam Ostrowski, department of public works superintendent. The cannon was ultimately turned over to the war effort. It was melted down and the metal was reused for weapons. The cannon had been a popular attraction at the park where children used to play on it. Although the cannon is now gone, the park looks essentially the same at it did in the war years, and children still play there.

While the labor movement remained cantankerous during the war, threatening strikes at Dodge Main or against the city at various times, the workers did their part for the war effort. By January 1942, Walter Serement (right), acting chairman of the labor division of the city's defense bond sales committee, reported that the union locals in Hamtramck had bought $200,000 in bonds. Cornelius Moll, financial secretary of United Automobile Workers of America Local 262, presents another bond purchase of $4,000 to Serement.

Members of the Spirit of Hamtramck Club are busy packing cigarettes to be shipped to the troops overseas in January 1943. More than 1,000 packages were sent out. Packing the smokes, from left to right, are (first row) Albert Zepke and Genevieve Kanski; (second row) Antoinette Liopnicki, Ignatius Nadolski, and Stanley Szyskiewicz.

Flags flew prominently in a parade on Jos. Campau Street in the early 1940s, possibly for Memorial Day. Parades were frequent events and always drew large crowds. North End Recreation, a two-level bowling alley in the background, places this north of Caniff Street. The American Legion was well-represented among the marchers. (Joseph Lucas collection.)

The Hamtramck Honor Roll was erected near the municipal building on Jos. Campau Street to list all Hamtramckans who joined the service. But after the draft was begun the list of names swelled. And as the sign became more weather-beaten, the city gave up trying to list everyone and repainted it with just the total number of soldiers—4,786 by June 1943.

Mayor Walter Kanar looks over the honor board that listed all the service men and women from Hamtramck. It was a source of pride for the city as more and more Hamtramckans went into the service.

In August 1942, the army was promoting the U.S. Army Air Corps as an option for men between ages 18 and 26 facing military service. To help spread the word about the air corps, Boy Scouts Emil Ewanovich (left) and John Kruszewski, under the direction of Helen Pietrzak, placed posters for the air corps in stores on Jos. Campau Street. Pietrzak was in charge of the Aviation Cadet Corps Recruiting Aides.

New nurses don their uniforms at St. Francis Hospital in August 1943. The war caused a critical shortage of nurses. To ease the need, congress passed the Bolton Act, which established a U.S. Nurse Cadet Corps, a unit of which operated at St. Francis, among hospitals nationwide.

Three

IN THE SERVICE

Many of them were hardly more than kids. Some rushed to join the military even before the war began. Others were drafted and hated every moment they spent in the military.

Hamtramckans turned out in huge numbers to fight the enemy. Nearly 7,000 served in the armed forces during the war. In virtually all cases, serving turned out to be the experience of a lifetime—for better or for worse. Suddenly boys who had never strayed far from home were being sent to faraway places ranging from New Guinea to Sicily. They went to lands they had never heard of before and often never wanted to see again. The fury of battle was nothing like anything anyone expected who had not experienced it before. It was brutal and terrifying even to the bravest. And they were brave. Experiencing the worst, they fought on and on. Capt. George Busher flew 163 strafing missions in Italy. Bomber crews flew multiple missions over Europe and in the Pacific. Sailors had their boats sunk from under them, infantrymen dodged bullets.

Some showed extraordinary courage. Like Lt. Raymond Zussman, who almost single-handedly liberated a village in France and was awarded a Congressional Medal of Honor—posthumously, as he was killed a short time after saving the town.

Many others did not return from the war. Nearly 200 would make the ultimate sacrifice, leaving grieving families and shattered homes that could never be made whole.

The war generated stories of great bravery and feelings of pride. But that came at a high price for those who served and their families.

Home for leave in March 1942, Lt. j.g. Charles Kovaleski was already a seasoned veteran. He was an officer aboard the U.S.S. *Yorktown* during an attack on the Gilbert Islands. As Kovaleski addressed the Hamtramck Rotary Club, Hamtramck High School principal E. M. Conklin (left) and school finance director Frank S. Sosnowski were on hand to greet him.

Lt. William Preston trained at Fort Sill, Oklahoma, before winning a full commission in field artillery just six months after entering the U.S. Army in June 1941.

Cadet Chester Gugala of the Naval Air Corps returned to Hamtramck in November 1942, serving as the guard of honor for Cadet Walter Krager. Gugala accompanied the body of Krager for burial back in Detroit. Krager had been killed in an air accident.

Not for men only: Stella Zadroga, third officer in the Women's Army Auxiliary Corps, returned to the Tau Beta Community House in October 1942 to meet with fellow members of the Junior Study Club. The club had been formed in 1930 to instill leadership and culture in its members. Meeting with her, from left to right, were club members Louise Ferenc, Ann Sorokin, Adele Aras, Mary Popyk, Jeanette O'Donnell, Wanda Skrat, and Anna Mae Ferenc.

John Warzywak, water tender first class, had been in the U.S. Navy for nearly 15 years before America entered the war. In October 1942, he returned home and made front page news by donating $25 to the city's war chest drive. With Warzywak are, from left to right, city employee union president Chester Reese, Mrs. Reese, and John's wife, Alice.

Pvt. Thaddeus Wagner (née Wojcichowski) was headed for glider school in September 1942 in Smyrna, Tennessee, when he came back home to Hamtramck on leave.

"I'm the third one in the first row," wrote Casimir Protasiewicz on a real-photo postcard sent home to Hamtramck in July 1944. Protasiewicz was stationed at Fort Sheridan, Illinois.

Midshipman Richard Krotkiewicz (second from left) marked his 21st birthday in July 1942 while on leave. With him at his home on Caniff Street, from left to right, are fellow midshipmen John Plawcha, Richard Pless, and Ted Jakubowski. All were midshipmen at Annapolis and headed back to the academy shortly after this photograph was taken.

Navy food was never like this. Annapolis midshipman Richard Krotkiewicz prepares to dig in during his visit home in July 1942. Holding the bottle at left is John Plawcha, and pouring is Ted Jakubowski.

"At home," wrote Cpl. Joseph Kowalski on this photograph from his base in Sacramento, California. The makeshift accommodations were typical of what soldiers experienced on bases all across the country. Note the World War I–style puttees he is wearing over his shoes.

AUTHORIZATION FOR ALLOTMENT OF PAY
(See AR 35–5520)

KOWALSKI	JOSEPH	A.	36104210	Corporal	Co.B, 749th M.P. Bn.
(Last name)	(First name)	(Middle initial)	(Army serial number)	(Grade)	(Company, regiment, or arm or service)

The *{officer / enlisted man} named above hereby authorizes a Class _____

allotment of his pay in the amount of $ **6.70** _____ per month for **Duration of War,** plus 6 months

(Type of allotment) months commencing

August 1, _____, 19 **43**, and expiring **after duration of War plus 6 months** _____, 19 ____

(**1**) premiums deducted from pay for month of **August** _____, 19 **43**

to **VETERANS ADMINISTRATION** (Applicable to Government insurance only (sec. IV, Cir. No. 100, W. D., 1942))

WASHINGTON D. C.

(Name of allotee)	(Number and street or rural route)	(City, town, or post office)	(State)
***	***	***	***

or to _____ **March 4,** _____ **41**

(Name of alternate allotee)	(Number and street or rural route)	(City, town, or post office)	(State)

Date of enlistment _____, 19 ____ When other than "Finance Service, Army" is affected,

state allotment chargeable **none** _____ Relationship of allotee ***

(Applicable to individual allotees only)

If allotment is in favor of a bank, the following is required to be stated: Deposit should be made to the credit of—

*** ****

(Name)	(Relationship)

(Statement below not applicable to Government insurance)

I hereby state that the purpose for which this allotment is granted is solely for the support of wife, child, or dependent relatives; or if made for the payment of life insurance premiums, the insurance (including endowments and/or twenty (or other) payment policies) is on the life of the allotter only; that the insurance constitutes the major and not a merely incidental or collateral element of the transaction; and that the allotment is made in favor of the insurance company issuing the policy and not in favor of a bank or other agent.

Place **Sacramento, California** _____

_____ _Joseph A. Kowalski_
(Signature of allotter)

Entered on service record **July 18, 1943** **July 15,** _____, 19 **43**
(Date) (Date)

* Strike out words not applicable.

CLIFFORD B. GRAHAM, 1st Lt., 749th MP. Bn. Ass't Adj.
(Signature of commanding or other personnel officer, with grade and organization)

WHEN APPLICABLE TO CLASS D OR CLASS N INSURANCE, THE ORIGINAL COPY OF THIS FORM WILL BE SENT TO THE EXAMINATION DIVISION, BUILDING X, 19TH AND B STREETS NE., WASHINGTON, D. C. NO COPIES WILL BE SENT TO THE VETERANS ADMINISTRATION, WASHINGTON, D. C., WITH THE APPLICATION FOR INSURANCE.

W. D., A. G. O. Form No. 29
November 4, 1942

16—0421-2   U. S. GOVERNMENT PRINTING OFFICE

Vertical text left margin: When applicable to Class E allotments, send original direct to the Disbursing Officer, Office of Dependency Benefits, 213 Washington Street, Newark, N. J.

An interesting sidelight of the service was the insurance premiums paid by soldiers to the Veterans Administration. Cpl. Joseph Kowalski paid $6.70 per month for the duration of the war, plus six months.

A soldier had two constant companions: his gun and his dog tags. These pressed-metal tags were worn around the neck and included vital information, including blood type. Often they were the only way to identify soldiers killed in battle and could prove vital in treating wounded soldiers who needed blood transfusions.

Sgt. Robert Buckley was hailed as a hero of Guadalcanal in October 1943. He was cited for "displaying superhuman courage and daring," in rallying the troops and turning back a Japanese attack.

The Newburn Coal and Supply Company did its patriotic duty by devoting most of its newspaper advertisement in the *Citizen* to promoting the WAVES. Ensign Helen Stewart, head of recruiting in Detroit for the WAVES, struck a stark pose for the promotion. The WAVES would fill in duties done by men, freeing them up for combat. The job paid a minimum of $50 a month.

Taking some time to relax, Sgt. Cass Copper (née Czyzewski) and his wife visited with city council president Walter Serement at Newland's Bar in October 1942.

Lou Stober was the center of attention when he returned to Hamtramck on leave in September 1942. Lou was feted at a party held in brother Dave's house. Dave Stober (right) operated a popular clothing store on Jos. Campau Street for many years. At left is Dave Widgerson, Dave Stober's business partner.

Seaman 2nd Class Edward Czarnecki (left) and Aviation Machinists Mate 3rd Class Ray Lempke survived the attack that sunk the aircraft carrier *Wasp* on September 15, 1942, off the Solomon Islands. "The three torpedoes struck at 2:30 p.m., an hour later we were ordered to abandon ship, and three hours we were picked up by a destroyer," they said.

Not all war casualties were the result of battles, 2nd Lt. Alfred Kuber died in November 1942 in a San Francisco hospital of a kidney aliment. His sister Emily was with him and returned to Hamtramck with his body.

Three unidentified local soldiers stationed in California show the typical uniform, complete with steel helmets, rifles, canteens, and backpacks.

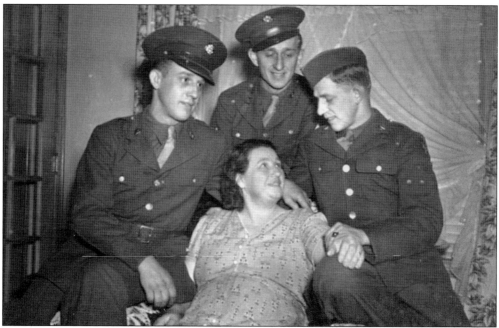

Home to visit their ailing father, Chester, William, and John Malinowski sit with their mother at their Moran Street home in January 1943. Chester (left) was with the Army Engineers, William (center) was with Army Ordinance, and John was with the Army Air Corps. Chester made the most of the trip, marrying Hattie Jankowski while on furlough.

These are typical patches, pins, and medals, which were common military wear. The bars at right indicated area of service. The medal is for good conduct.

Pvt. Joseph Wojcikowski returned home on furlough in January 1943. He then returned to Camp Crowder in Missouri where he was studying to be an electrician.

NOTICE OF CLASSIFICATION App. not Req.

Joseph (First name) George (Middle name) Tabor (Last name)

Order No. 2387 has been classified in Class 2-B

(Until 2-24-1945, 19)
(Insert date for Class II-A and II-B only)

by ☒ Local Board.
☐ Board of Appeal (by vote of ____ to ____).
☐ President.

8-24-1944 19 Robert Duckman
(Date of mailing) (member of local board)

The law requires notice, in addition to possession at all times surrender it, upon en... DSS Form 57. (Rev...

Jos. G. Tabor, W8AES
19215 Westphalia Ave.,
Detroit 5, Michigan

...lation, to have this ...2), in your personal ...horized officials—to ...manding officer.

The dreaded draft card: every man who registered for the draft received a card with various classifications. Joseph George Tabor was a 2-B, an occupational deferment. But no one wanted a 4-F. While that would keep one out of the army, many saw it as a stigma that the person was physically unfit for service, usually because of a medical condition. And if one was not fit for the army, some questioned whether they were fit to be hired for a job.

This barracks in a base in California is typical of the quarters the soldiers from Hamtramck encountered when they went into training before being shipped overseas.

RAYMOND ZUSSMAN
Second Lieutenant
U.S. Army, 756th Tank Battalion

MEDAL OF HONOR RECIPIENT
POSTHUMOUS AWARD
Noroy le Bourg, France
12 September 1944

Hamtramck's proudest moment took place across the Atlantic with the heroic actions of 2nd Lt. Raymond Zussman. With the U.S. Army 756th Tank Battalion on September 12, 1944, Zussman was in command of two tanks and an infantry company in an attack on Noroy le Bourg, France. With one tank bogged down, he advanced alone, returning numerous times to direct fire on enemy positions. Coming under fire from machine guns, Zussman stood his ground, leading his remaining tank. His actions led to the killing of 18 and capture of 92 German soldiers. Just days later he was killed in action. For his bravery he was awarded the Congressional Medal of Honor—Hamtramck's only Medal of Honor recipient. His heroism was commemorated with this special envelope issued for Veterans Day in 2002.

Frank Stock was on his way to church in Hawaii on December 7, 1941, when he saw three Japanese planes heading toward Pearl Harbor. He rushed to his ship, grabbed a 30 caliber gun and began firing. "I didn't hit anything, but I kept firing away," he said. In July 1944, he returned home for leave and was greeted by his mother and family.

Sgt. Bill Burns was honorably discharged from the U.S. Army in September 1943 after seeing combat in New Guinea. Headed for civilian life, he checks out a new suit from his former boss, Bill Harrison, of Harrison clothing store on East Davison Street.

Richard Wilhelm served in the Coast Guard, stationed in San Francisco in 1943.

Sgt. Harry Prazuch related tales of Pearl Harbor when he returned home on leave in August 1943. Prazuch witnessed the attack firsthand. He told his story to city councilman Frank Sosnowski; Prazuch's father, Andrew; and councilman John Anger. The visit was his first trip home in four years.

On Harry Kulchesky's 25th bombing raid over Germany his plane was hit by enemy fire in September 1943. With the bomb bay door jammed, a fire inside, and two engines knocked out of action, the plane limped back to England. To make matters worse, the landing gear jammed and the plane had to make a belly landing, skidding a mile through a mass of barbed wire. Kulchesky emerged unharmed.

Chester "Boots" Reese got some support from the troops in January 1944 when two servicemen home on leave took out nominating petitions for him as he ran for the city council. Reese was president of the city workers' Congress of Industrial Organizations (CIO) Local 257. Getting petitions from Charles Lark of the city clerk's office are Marine corporal Joseph Warzwak and Merchant Marine Joseph Jagodzinski. The effort was in vain. Reese lost.

The enigmatic epitaph "Honor and Justice Prevailed" adorns the gravestone of Pvt. Eddie Slovik. Slovik, who lived on Edwin Street and attended Dickinson School, was the only soldier executed for desertion in World War II. In fact, he was the first soldier executed for desertion since the Civil War. Slovik left his post twice, and his punishment was seen as a deterrent to any would-be deserters. To this day his death remains controversial, as he was the only one of more than 21,000 soldiers charged with desertion to be executed. He lies beside his wife, Antoinette, in Detroit's Woodmere Cemetery. Her stone bears the poignant legend "Compassion and Justice unto this Moment Unfulfilled." Today there is a movement to restore Slovik's reputation by those who feel his punishment was too harsh.

Walter Jarocki (right) came home on leave from the Coast Guard in February 1944 just in time to bid farewell to his friend Eugene Kowalski, who was going to the University of Illinois to begin studying under the Army Specialized Training Program.

Cpl. Hugh Brass brought an interesting perspective of the war to his father, Julius Brass, owner of Progressive Cleaners. Hugh was a member of the military police guarding German prisoners of war in Victoria, Arkansas. He noted that there were "Germans" and "Nazis," the former being decent men, and the latter cocky enemies convinced the Nazis would win and the war would be over by Christmas 1943, when this photograph was taken.

As the war progressed, the tales told by the servicemen became more harrowing. Pfc. Walter Imbirowicz (right) relates his story of drawing the fire of Japanese troops as his company advanced on the Pacific island of Attu. Shot in the arm, he returned home in August 1943 and told his story to seaman Stanley Achram and Tony Bartkowicz, who was awaiting induction into the army.

Water Tender 1st Class John Schuller logged 200,000 miles on a heavy cruiser in five years of service. Schuller saw action at such diverse places as Casablanca, Guadalcanal, Attu, Kiska, and was part of a convoy to Murmansk.

This postcard of a French church was sent from the war zone in March 1945. "It's been too cold to write. I'll send you a letter some day soon," Cpl. Jimmy Robertson wrote. The card was duly passed and stamped by the U.S. Army Examiner.

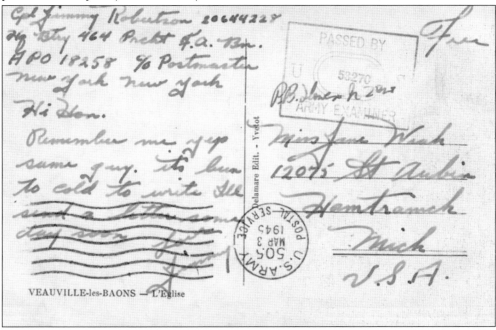

It took 22 years, but former staff sergeant Walter Markiewicz finally received official notification that he had won a Bronze Start for "Meritorious Achievement" in the European Theater of Operations in 1944. For some reason, Markiewicz was not informed that he had been approved to receive the medal until February 1966.

Cpl. John Targosz was the city's first casualty. Targosz, 20, was a marine when he was killed in action on September 12, 1942, in the Solomon Islands in the Pacific.

In Memory of

CPL. JOHN TARGOSZ

November 16, 1921 - September 12, 1942

First Hamtramck resident to die in World War II

✝

Our heavenly Father, the souls of our comrades are in your presence. They have served their country proudly.

Touch them gently, as they have touched our lives in the fight for freedom.

Our comrades have sailed the seas, flown in the clouds, and walked the earth in battle so we may have a better life.

We will forever cherish their memory, for they are yours in heaven for eternity. Eternal rest grant them forever and ever.   Amen.

Eddie Borycz had an incredible tale to tell when he returned home in December 1943. He and a friend saw action in Agregento, Sicily, where they captured eight Nazi tanks, 6,000 prisoners, and 2,000 rifles. Borycz survived being blown up by a mortar shell that ripped his back open. He was sent home on medical leave and related his story to Eddie Kozaren at Johnny Lega's bar on Jos. Campau Street.

After more than two years overseas, mainly at Pago Pago Island in the South Pacific, Marine corporal Marion Kadykowski came home on leave—with a string of battle and service ribbons in February 1944. He was in the coast artillery and was awarded ribbons for service prior to the attack on Pearl Harbor for proficiency with five weapons.

Surrounded by Japanese soldiers on New Guinea, Pvt. Thomas Gesinski dropped to 89 pounds subsisting on Argentinean chicken and spoonfuls of rice. He suffered a concussion from a shrapnel blast as Allied troops came to the rescue and was awarded a Purple Heart. On returning home in May 1943, his coworkers at the Falls Spring and Wire plant plied him with cake and food favorites, like kielbasa. Plant manager Steve Azarvitz assured him that his job was waiting when he returned.

Four

LIFE GOES ON

While the war worked its way into nearly every facet of life, it was not all-consuming. It could not be. People had to go to work, kids went to school, churches held services, and people went to the movies. And it was politics as usual, at least in the early years of the war as Hamtramck's political scene was marked by the usual squabbling and infighting.

Still, things were being done. Work was completed on Immaculate Conception Ukrainian Catholic Church in 1942, just beating the wartime shortage of building materials. The city bought new rubbish hauling trucks in 1942. At about the same time, thieves robbed $1,500 from the Bowery night club. The Goodfellows collected $5,232 in its Christmas drive in 1942.

In January 1943, the public school teachers staged a three-day strike seeking a pay raise. And 14 young men wearing zoot suits were hauled into court in February 1943 for causing a ruckus in a bar on Conant Street. In April 1944, Mayor Stephen Skrzycki easily won a second term, defeating former mayor Joseph Lewandowski, 6,711 to 4,229 votes. In the same election Albert Zak, who became one of Hamtramck's most venerable politicians, was elected to a third term as city clerk.

And one day in October 1942, Hamtramck took on tones of a war zone itself when a locomotive plowed into a crowded bus as it crossed the tracks west of Caniff Street. Sixteen were killed, their bodies torn apart and scattered for two blocks down the tracks. Forty-three others were injured in one of the worst accidents in Michigan's history.

The end of the war in Europe in May 1945 was welcomed quietly in Hamtramck, because everyone knew there was still much more fighting ahead. But it was a different situation the following August when the Japanese surrendered. Thousands of residents poured into the streets in a wild, but remarkably peaceful celebration.

Plans were made to welcome home the soldiers and sailors, some of whom had spent five years in the service. Families were joyously being reunited, but there were many challenges ahead as the returning veterans were faced with the difficulty of finding jobs in the scaled-back peacetime economy.

But they were coming home. And that was the only thing that really mattered.

Patriotism played a role in the Christmas party at Max's Jewelry in December 1941. America was freshly at war, facing an uncertain future. Saluting the flag are, from left to right, Herbert Rosenbaum, Max Rosenbaum, Mrs. Rosenbaum, and Bernice Rosenbaum.

"Dad" Benedict Krotkiewicz celebrated his 72nd birthday in grand style in March 1942. The owner of the popular Dad's Delicatessen was presented with flowers and a singing telegram. Bringing gifts are his son Edmund Krotkiewicz, secretary Zenia Wasiakowski, and daughter Elaine Krotkiewicz.

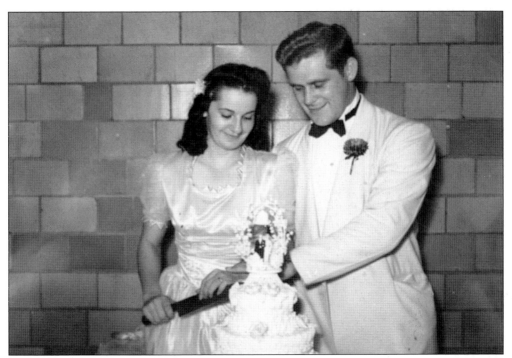

Some things were more important than the war, at least on certain days. In September 1942, Regina Piotrowski and Art Macioszczyk were married at St. Florian Church.

When Cpl. Henry Banas came home on furlough from North Africa in April 1944 he wed Marcy Junga at Our Lady Queen of Heaven Church. It was not unusual for soldiers to get married while on leave.

A full year into the war, Dave Stober and staff issued a Christmas greeting to all the loyal customers who made his clothing store on Jos. Campau Street one of the most successful in Hamtramck. "Thank you for your patronage and your patience during a year marked by shortages, rationing and so on," they stated. The staff members are (first row) Ed Applin, Rita Ceifetz, Dave Stober, Dr. Jack Ecker, and Jacob Talik; (second row) Nick Laptue, Hank Ruby, Ed Astemborski, Stanley Dombrowski, and Isadore Levinthal.

Going to the movies, frequent dances, and sports activities were recreational options during the war years. In November 1942, Emil Dimitri was one of the many who enjoyed bowling at North End Recreation, which was noted for its two levels of bowling alleys.

The Baker Street Car rolls down Jos. Campau Street near Caniff Street in 1942. The Martha Washington Theatre, at right, was a popular stop. During the war years, before television, people often went to the movies three and four times a week.

Some 8,000 people turned out for the big football game between Detroit Catholic Central and Hamtramck High School on October 2, 1942. Among the guests was Gov. Murray Van Wagoner, seated next to Mayor Stephen Skrzycki. They are in the second row, Van Wagoner with the white hat and Skrzycki with the dark one. Unfortunately Hamtramck was clobbered 46-0.

Holbrook Street west of St. Aubin Street was a narrow lane in February 1943. But on either side of street stood the Chevrolet Gear and Axle plant buildings, which also had shifted to war production.

Albert Zak was elected city clerk in 1940 with a promise of streamlining operations. He did in July 1942 when he introduced the new business license form, which actually encompassed 44 different licenses on one sheet. At that time, businesses had to have as many as seven licenses to operate. Zak combined them onto one simple form. Smiling approvingly is councilman John Wojtylo.

The staff of Max's Jewelry store gathered for their first Christmas at war on December 23, 1941. Max's remained one of Hamtramck's most popular businesses for decades.

Members of the Hamtramck Police Department gathered for a photograph on September 22, 1943. They had plenty to keep them busy. At about the time this picture was taken, the police made their biggest gambling raid ever, confiscating a roomful of gambling paraphernalia from an office on Goodson Street.

The gift of life arrived even as death overwhelmed the world. In January 1943, John Pitlosh watched over his newborn daughter beneath the Christmas tree in their home on Edwin Street.

Domestic automobile manufacturing stopped soon after the war began and factories switched to military vehicle production. But that did not mean there were no more cars on the road. In May 1943, department of public works employees produced a city's worth of parking signs.

New trees are planted on Gallagher Street north of Caniff Street in May 1943. The street looks much the same today, although these trees probably fell victim to Dutch elm disease, which rampantly killed millions of trees in the 1940s and 1950s.

Founded in 1934, the *Citizen* has been Hamtramck's newspaper of record ever since. During the war years it was especially popular in bringing the hometown news to the soldiers overseas. In February 1943, soldiers on leave (from left to right) Cpl. John Kaczor, stationed in the Panama Canal zone, and Pfc. Joseph Marcinkowski and Pfc. Joseph Kulaszewicz, both stationed at Fort MacArthur, California, stopped by the Citizen office to show their appreciation of the paper.

Trouble erupted on the home front at 10:27 a.m. Tuesday, July 17, 1943, at the Johnson Milk Company at Caniff Street and Gallagher Street. Some 300 member of the CIO descended on 25 rival American Federation of Labor picketers. The 15-minute melee that resulted included the firing of several shots. More than a dozen picketers and police were injured. The two unions were disputing who had the contract to represent the workers.

Even as the United States prepared to engage in the war, workers for the city of Hamtramck were fighting for better conditions and job security. In January 1942, Mayor Walter Kanar signed a new contract with the city employees, represented by department of public works superintendent Fred Pabst (center) and Ross Baker, business agent for the city workers' union.

WAR RATION BOOK No. 3   Void if altered

309090LL

NOT VALID WITHOUT STAMP

Identification of person to whom issued: PRINT IN FULL

James Kowalski

(First name)   (Middle name)   (Last name)

Street number or rural route   *2253 Wyandotte*

City or post office   *Hamtk.*   State   *Mich.*

AGE	SEX	WEIGHT Lbs.	HEIGHT Ft. In.	OCCUPATION

SIGNATURE   *James Kowalski*

(Person to whom book is issued. If such person is unable to sign because of age or incapacity, another may sign in his behalf.)

WARNING

This book is the property of the United States Government. It is unlawful to sell it to any other person, or to use it or permit anyone else to use it, except to obtain rationed goods in accordance with regulations of the Office of Price Administration. Any person who finds a lost War Ration Book must return it to the War Price and Rationing Board which issued it. Persons who violate rationing regu-

LOCAL BOARD ACTION

Issued by _____

(Local board number)   (Date)

Street address _____

City _____   State _____

Sugar, flour, gasoline, meat, even whiskey were in short supply during the war. Ration books limiting the amount of items a family could purchase became commonplace. "If you don't need it—don't buy it," the government intoned. But some folks were driven to such desperation they traded their food allotment stamps to increase their liquor stipend.

Hamtramck High School football coach Floyd Stocum, who became legendary in local sports, surveys the field and the upcoming season on September 1942. With him are team captains Chester Tzay (left) and Mitchell Berlin. High on their "hit list" was perennial rival Detroit Catholic Central.

Emerging from a chaotic political battlefield, Dr. Stephen Skrzycki was elected mayor in April 1942. He was sworn in by city clerk Albert Zak at the municipal offices. His first task was to address the city's $6.8 million debt. Financial problems would plague Hamtramck long after Skrzycki was gone.

Even with war shortages it was still possible to get some major projects accomplished. By February 1942, the city was ready to begin expanding Gallagher Street through the block from Evaline Avenue to Caniff Street.

On Friday, July 24, 1942, the work on Gallagher Street was completed and opened with a ribbon-cutting ceremony. Mayor Stephen Skrzycki cut the ribbon. Among those participating was councilman Joseph Sawicki (left).

What city construction projects that were done through the war years generally were overseen by I. M. Kopkowski, city engineer. Kopkowski was associated with the city for many years. He is shown here at his office in June 1942.

Fund-raising efforts were not confined to war bonds and stamps. In March 1943, Mayor Stephen Skrzycki (left), city councilman Frank Sosnowski (center), and assistant school superintendent Stanley Biernacki were among the first to buy the season's Easter Seals. Proceeds from the sale were used to support local, state, and national programs to aid crippled children.

Tennis legend Jean Hoxie was already coaching champions in July 1944. Prior to heading to Milwaukee for the Western Junior Boys and Girls Tournament, Hoxie practiced with Dick Russell and Johnny Koliba (in front of net) and Al Hetzeck and Walter Russell (behind net). Hoxie led the Hamtramck players to international recognition and was featured in a 1948 edition of the *Reader's Digest*.

Woodrow W. Woody opened his Pontiac dealership on Jos. Campau Street in 1940. Despite the shortages wrought by Word War II, and despite the fact Hamtramck was a solidly Dodge town, thanks to the Dodge Main plant, Woody Pontiac grew to be the No. 1 Pontiac dealership in the nation. Woody remained active in his business and the community almost until he died in 2002 at age 94. (Joseph Lucas collection.)

War notwithstanding, the democratic process went on. The election of 1942 drew a high turnout, but was noted for its serenity compared to previous elections. Dr. Stephen Skrzycki emerged as the front runner in the primary of March 1942 and would go on to win the general election. Looking over the voter registration ranks are, from left to right, Ordine Tolliver, city clerk Albert Zak, and August Lang.

Hamtramck was led through the war years by two mayors: Walter Kanar and Dr. Stephen Skrzycki. A controversial figure, Kanar was first elected to the Michigan legislature in 1931 and to the Hamtramck City Council in 1936. In 1939, when Mayor Rudolph Tenerowicz resigned to run for congress, Kanar was named mayor by the council. He won the election in 1940 but resigned in 1942 amid an investigation that he accepted kickbacks.

Dr. Stephen Skrzycki was elected mayor in 1942—despite sporting a mustache that made him look somewhat similar to another news maker of the time. Skrzycki's 10 years in office marked a new period of Hamtramck politics when charges of corruption were noticeably absent. When he died in 1954—the first Hamtramck mayor to die—thousands turned out for his funeral.

Despite the smiles, it was a somber day when Mayor Walter Kanar resigned and turned over the keys to his office to Anthony Tenerowicz. Tenerowicz, brother of former mayor Rudolph Tenerowicz, was council president and served briefly as acting mayor in early 1942.

Mayor Stephen Skrzycki makes his inaugural address in April 1942 at the city council chambers. Skrzycki had his battles with the city unions, but his 10-year tenure was extraordinarily quiet in comparison to previous administrations.

By September 1942, thousands of Hamtramckans were in the service. To commemorate that fact, the city workers' union presented a banner to the city. The red, white, and blue banner on a field of blue stars actually carried too high a number. Selective service said Hamtramck had "only" 2,300 men and women in the service, but was expected to reach 2,900 by the end of 1942. Taking part in the presentation are, from left to right, employee union president Chester Reese, councilman Frank Sosnowski, Mayor Stephen Skrzycki, and special guest Johnny Gorsica, pitcher for the Detroit Tigers who was visiting the city.

Sheriff Andrew Baird paid a visit to Hamtramck in June 1942 when the Andy Baird Old Timers met at Vincent Sadlowski Imperial Cafe on Jos. Campau Street. Virtually all of Hamtramck's political elite turned out for the event, which included the presentation of a bowling trophy from Baird to team captain Frank Nowak. Also participating were councilman Frank Sosnowski (left) and Mayor Stephen Skrzycki.

Crosstown rivals St. Florian and St. Ladislaus found common ground at the Tau Beta Community House in December 1943. The players from the schools' football squads were honored at a party sponsored by the Kiwanis Club. Seen here, from left to right, are (first row) Art Curtis, program general chairman; J. Fred Lawton, speaker at the event; and Fr. A. Majewski, of St. Ladislaus; (second row) C. James Reid, originator of the annual school banquet, and Stan Nestorek, Cosmos ace back.

Here tennis coach Jean Hoxie encourages two of her stars who were finalists in the Hamtramck Open Michigan Girls Tennis Tournament in September 1943. Stephanie Prychitko (left) and Gloria King were part of Hoxie's stable of tennis champs.

Although there were shortages, Hamtramck businesses operated as well as they could. In December 1941, Julius Brass of Progressive Cleaners on Jos. Campau Street modernized his business. Clerk Helen Dombrowski approves of the new look.

City council president Walter Serement tries out the pole at the fire station in May 1943, possibly during an open house event.

OUR CHURCH

Commor Avenue   Between Charest and McDougall

Dedication Ceremony and Solemn Mass

PROGRAM

8:30 A. M.   Assembly of Organizations and Groups (near Church on Grayling Avenue)

9:00 A. M.   Procession begins.

9:45 A. M.   Dedication Ceremonies at the New Church.

10:00 A. M.   Solemn Mass.

1:00 P. M.   Banquet at the Ukrainian Hall, 2240 Grayling Ave.

Note: In case of rain there will be no parade.

On May 30, 1942—Memorial Day—Immaculate Conception Ukrainian Catholic Church was dedicated. It was the last major building project completed in Hamtramck until after World War II. Built with $160,000 raised by parishioners, it just beat the war shortage of materials. It stands virtually unchanged from the day it was dedicated on Commor Street.

In 1941, construction began on the Col. Hamtramck Housing units on Dequindre Street. The units were designed to provide low-cost, decent housing. The project quickly became embroiled in controversy, however, when the housing commission sought to reserve the units for white residents only, despite support for African American housing rights from some white Hamtramck residents. A 10-year court case resulted in the full integration of the units. (Joseph Lucas collection.)

City councilman Walter Serement inspects one of the 300 units in the Col. Hamtramck Housing project in February 1942, just as residents were getting ready to move in. To show how inexpensively the units could be furnished the Tau Beta Community House, Goodwill Industries and Federal Furniture Company supplied furniture. Total cost for completely furnishing a unit was $183.

DO YOU KNOW

THESE FACTS ABOUT
COL. HAMTRAMCK HOMES

300 NEW HOMES FOR RENT

YOUR LOW RENT WILL INCLUDE:
HEAT, ELECTRICITY, GAS AND WATER BILLS

**GAS RANGE
REFRIGERATOR
AUTOMATIC WATER HEATER
FURNISHED IN EACH HOME**

DO YOU KNOW ?

1. Children are welcome.
2. Playgrounds are on the site.
3. Each home will have a front and back yard.
4. Your relatives and friends may visit you.
5. Lights will not be turned out.
6. The home will be yours, and you will have all the rights that are a part of the American Way of Living.

APPLICATIONS NOW TAKEN

COL. HAMTRAMCK HOMES
TENANT SELECTION OFFICE
8550 JOS. CAMPAU AVE.
TELEPHONE TR. 2-7186

Hours: 8:30 A. M. — 4:30 P. M.
Daily

Tuesday: open to 9:00 P. M.
Saturday: open to 12:00 Noon

Utilities, gas range, refrigerator, automatic water heater—the Col. Hamtramck homes had the latest amenities for 1942 when the announcement went out that renters were being sought.

Edward Everett Horton was a major Hollywood character actor for many years. In May 1942, he stopped by Hamtramck High School to meet with the students. Horton was appearing in the play *Springtime for Henry* at the Shubert-Lafayette Theater.

Congressman (and former mayor) Rudolph Tenerowicz presented awards to four players who competed in the Hamtramck Open Tennis Tournament in August 1942. From left to right are Bill Garner of Catholic Central High School, winner of the boys singles title; Billy Sagan, runner-up; Hobart Wrobel, of Detroit, senior singles runner-up; Gene Russell, senior champ; Tenerowicz; and Jean Hoxie, Hamtramck tennis director.

A year into the war, phonograph records were still available and a popular form of entertainment. One of the best places to get them was Bejnar's store on Jos. Campau Street. Irene Pastuszka and Barbara Romaszko were in charge of the record department in December 1942. Bejnar's carried a wide variety of records including Polish, Slovak, Ukrainian, Russian, Hungarian, Serbian, Croatian, and Lithuanian records.

Copernicus Junior High School stands amid the snow in the winter of 1943. Note how few cars are present. The school, now Hamtramck High School, is still in operation and looks virtually unchanged today.

The Bowery was one of the leading night clubs in the Midwest through the 1940s and in the early 1950s. The Bowery was known nationally for bringing in top acts of the era. Sophie Tucker, Gypsy Rose Lee, the Three Stooges, Danny Thomas, and many others performed at the Bowery. Owner Frank Barbaro was a local celebrity himself. When he and his wife divorced in the early 1950s, she got the Bowery, and it closed a few years later. The Bowery was located on Jos. Campau Street.

Sophie Tucker was the "Last of the Red Hot Mamas," and she showed the style that made her a major singing sensation for decades at the Bowery. John Frankensteen is on the left and Walter Reuther is on the right. Both were leaders of the United Auto Workers.

Al's Cut Rate Hardware on Conant Street near Caniff Street was a popular place to shop during the war years. It is pictured here in October 1942.

While there were many shortages during the war, some amenities were still available. Atlas Furs on Jos. Campau Street shows a full line of products in the store windows in August 1942.

MARGOLIS FURNITURE CO.
9130 Jos. Campau, Detroit 12, Michigan. TR-inity 1-1500
Branch 5560 Chene Street. WA-lnut 1-9756

Wartime shortages aside, people did buy goods for their homes. Margolis furniture on Jos. Campau Street was the place that most Hamtramckans bought their furniture. In June 1942, Henry Kowalczyk spent $29.95 on an item.

Venerable Carpenter School was doomed in September 1943 when the school board voted to demolish the building. The move was designed to save the district some $25,000 in operating expenses. "We're economizing," school trustee Edward Kopek said. Soon it was reduced to a pile of rubble.

Youngsters try their hands at basket making in one of the many school programs that kept kids active in the 1940s.

A girl gets assistance working out in one of the school district's swimming pools. Along with recreational uses, pools were used for such specialized services as therapeutic treatments. This was especially important as the threat of polio was real and often devastating. The crippling, sometimes fatal disease, struck often until the mid-1950s when the polio vaccine was developed. But until that development there were times when the schools had to close because of polio outbreaks. Newspapers of the period are filled with heartbreaking stories of children crippled or killed by the disease.

The school pools were not used strictly for therapeutic needs. Here a group of residents looks over one of the pools, which were open to the public and provided a comfortable break in summer and winter.

Girls gather to play in a recreation department–sponsored activity at one of the schools in 1942. Recreation programs were a principal source of amusement for kids during the war years.

Civic pride and cleanliness were the lessons of the day for school kids in May 1944. The messages being displayed stressed cleanliness and that the proper place to walk was on sidewalks, not yards or grass. Note the inkwell holders on the old-style desks.

A full-page advertisement in the *Citizen* newspaper in April 1943 reminded all that the second war loan drive was to start shortly and that $13 billion had to be raised. Throughout the war, such advertisements and announcements of war bond drives were common as the government strove to raise money for the war effort.

Built in 1928, the Tau Beta Community House provided a host of services for many years including social services and recreational activities like dances, plays, and crafts. During the World War II years, the building was the site of Red Cross blood drives.

Five

IN THE AFTERMATH

Hamtramck exploded into a wild celebration at 7:00 p.m. Tuesday, August 15, 1945. That was the moment that Pres. Harry Truman made a radio announcement that the Japanese had surrendered. World War II was over.

A new chapter in Hamtramck's history was just beginning. Soon the soldiers would begin returning home. The ranks of the unemployed swelled as industry suddenly downsized while government orders for war material evaporated. But that situation would not last long. The money saved over the war years and the demand for new cars, appliances, and even homes reenergized the economy. But nothing would be the same again. The soldiers coming home had seen the world and were not content with the homes they had left behind. They wanted more space, more cars, more of everything. The exodus of people from Hamtramck, which had begun occurring in the mid-1930s, picked up after the war years as people began to move to the suburbs. Warren, Sterling Heights, Utica, Troy, and other towns with space for large lawns, big houses with garages, and driveways beckoned. It would not be until the 1990s that Hamtramck's population trend reversed again with new growth.

In 1979, Dodge Main closed and the Poles, who once made up the overwhelming majority of residents, dwindled to only 23 percent by 2006. New ethnic groups were moving into town, bringing their culture and identity to the town.

But one thing that would remain unchanged was the dynamic spirit of the community. A spirit that was implanted by the great influx of immigrants that turned Hamtramck into a major city after 1910.

Pres. Harry S. Truman became the second president (Franklin D. Roosevelt was the first) to visit Hamtramck when he visited the city on a campaign swing in September 1948. Some 20,000 people turned out to see Truman at Veterans Memorial Park. Many Hamtramckans had high hopes that the president could help save Poland from the grasp of the Communists, but that was not to be.

Bess Truman, wife of Pres. Harry Truman, receives a bouquet of flowers as she visits Hamtramck with her husband in 1948. The Trumans had affection for Hamtramck. Although Bess rode in the car, the president walked down Jos. Campau Street. The Trumans visited Hamtramck several times.

After an initial economic slump as the ranks of the unemployed were swelled by returning soldiers, a pent-up demand for new cars quickly got the assembly lines rolling again. Dodge Main soon was churning out cars, which crowded around the streets of the plant once the war was finally over.

Woodrow W. Woody was a benefactor of the upswinging economy. Building on the economic prosperity of the postwar years, he used his savvy business sense to build Woody Pontiac to one of the most successful car dealerships in the nation. Woody also had a strong sense of the community and was instrumental in building the Hamtramck Public Library building on Caniff Street.

The postwar years brought many changes. There was a sense of newness, as shown by the Pure Food Supermarket, one of two that operated on Jos. Campau Street. It was part of the trend that replaced the corner stores that once peppered the community. The new concept got a new look with modern siding.

Pure Food's wide aisles, abundant products and self-service were the hallmarks of the new supermarkets that were springing up all across America, including Hamtramck.

Long after Prohibition ended, illegal stills were bubbling up in Hamtramck. From time to time in the late 1940s, police would raid stores and homes in the city where they would uncover moonshine operations, Hamtramck-style. This setup was uncovered in one building in about 1947.

The public schools were embroiled in turmoil after World War II. In 1948, a movement was begun to oust school board trustees Stephen Sulczewski, Anthony Kar, Walter Pluzdrak, and John Lewandowski amid charges that money was embezzled and Kar was the "chief schemer and plotter behind it."

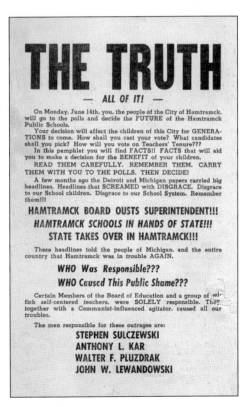

THE TRUTH

— ALL OF IT! —

On Monday, June 14th, you, the people of the City of Hamtramck, will go to the polls and decide the FUTURE of the Hamtramck Public Schools.

Your decision will affect the children of this City for GENERATIONS to come. How shall you cast your vote? What candidates shall you pick? How will you vote on Teachers' Tenure???

In this pamphlet you will find FACTS!! FACTS that will aid you to make a decision for the BENEFIT of your children.

READ THEM CAREFULLY. REMEMBER THEM. CARRY THEM WITH YOU TO THE POLLS. THEN DECIDE!

A few months ago the Detroit and Michigan papers carried big headlines. Headlines that SCREAMED with DISGRACE. Disgrace to our School children. Disgrace to our School System. Remember them!!!

HAMTRAMCK BOARD OUSTS SUPERINTENDENT!!!

HAMTRAMCK SCHOOLS IN HANDS OF STATE!!!

STATE TAKES OVER IN HAMTRAMCK!!!

These headlines told the people of Michigan, and the entire country that Hamtramck was in trouble AGAIN.

WHO Was Responsible???

WHO Caused This Public Shame???

Certain Members of the Board of Education and a group of self-ish self-centered teachers, were SOLELY responsible. They together with a Communist-influenced agitator, caused all our troubles.

The men responsible for these outrages are:

STEPHEN SULCZEWSKI
ANTHONY L. KAR
WALTER F. PLUZDRAK
JOHN W. LEWANDOWSKI

119

The Blue Star Mothers of America and the American Gold Star Mothers trace their origins to World War I when women who had relatives in the service began wearing blue stars on their left arms. As casualties increased, the women added a gold star over the blue for loved ones lost in the war.

Two gold star mothers carry a wreath to be laid at the veterans monument at Veterans Memorial Park in a post–World War II Memorial Day parade. Hedwig Tomaszewski's son served in World War II and later in the Korean War where he died of starvation in a prisoner of war camp. She is on the left. On the right is Mary Wojcinski, whose son died in World War II.

Amid the war-time bustle it seemed unimaginable that Dodge Main might one day close. But the world was a different place by 1979 when the Chrysler Corporation teetered on bankruptcy, and Dodge Main shutdown forever. A year later, it was reduced to rubble, then obliterated to make room for a new General Motors plant. Dodge Main is now just a memory, replaced by the General Motors Detroit-Hamtramck Assembly Plant.

Eighty-five percent of Hamtramck's houses were built between 1915 and 1930. By the end of World War II, their age was showing. While this house on Yemans Street was an extreme case, there were others scattered around town. Following the war there was a national effort to rebuild towns through urban renewal programs. Many old houses were razed or renovated. But that could not stop the drain of residents who increasingly moved to the suburbs after the war. That trend finally reversed in the 1990s.

City councilwoman Julia Rooks makes a donation to the poppy drive being conducted by the Disabled American Veterans during the 1950s. Following the war, various veteran groups, including the Veterans of Foreign Wars, Polish League of American Veterans, American Legion, and their auxiliaries, were thriving in Hamtramck.

In the wake of the war, soldiers and their vehicles took an even more prominent role in the plethora of parades the city held. This armored vehicle rolled down Jos. Campau Street for the Thanksgiving Day parade in November 1962.

Civilian defense remained a legacy of the war, only there was a new enemy to be faced—the Communists. The iron curtain that descended on Europe after World War II ushered in the Cold War. The Federal Office of Civilian Defense ended in 1945 and was succeeded by the Federal Civil Defense program, which focused on dealing with the threat of nuclear attacks. Here Mayor Albert Zak (right) looks over a rescue and service truck in the early 1950s.

Zak (far right), mayor-to-be William Kozerski (second from right), and school superintendent E. M. Conklin stand with an unidentified member of the Hamtramck Allied Veterans Council and the council's flag. Veterans' groups took on a great role in the city's social and political scene after the war.

The spirit of patriotism became deeply embedded in Hamtramck following the war years. Memorial Day ceremonies drew huge crowds. Numerous veterans groups opened halls in the city and participated in city events.

Ultimately it all came to this—the American flag held by Mayor Al Zak—and all it stands for.

"In grateful tribute" Hamtramck remembers all who made the ultimate sacrifice for freedom. The names of all Hamtramck soldiers who died in the nation's wars are engraved on the monument at Veterans Memorial Park.

THE ULTIMATE SACRIFICE

The following soldiers from Hamtramck died for the country in World War II.

John A. Anderson
Casmere W. Bagnowski
Joseph Baldyga
Arthur J. Bank
Leonard Barbieri
James Barna
Thaddeus H. Benachowski
Leo Bender
Alfred T. Biel
Casmere R. Bielecki
Hary Biesiadecki
Casmere Blaszczyk
Teddy J. Blezien
Alphonse Brzozowski
John Bublavi
Felix Bush
Joseph Bywalec
Julian B. Cosarz
Felix Cetner
Raymond M. Cichoracki
Berline Cipresso
Joseph E. Cwiek
Raymond P. Cywinski
Julius Czerwinski
Edward J. Darlak
Michael Dmytryszym
Raymond C. Dolenga
Frank J. Dravetsky
John Dureno Jr.
Edward Dyczewski

Stanislaus F. Dylewski
Joseph Dziedzic
John Enko
John C. Fedorowicz
Walter Fedorow
Joe F. Filip
Henry Florczak
Jerome J. Gagala
Joseph Gapinski
John Gardel
James L. Gibbs
Steve Glaub
Bruno Golinski
Eugene Gontarz
Steve L. Gorgal
Joseph Gryniewicz
Raymond D. Grzenkowicz
Frank S. Gubala
Walter Gurnicz
Anthony Habas
Joseph A. Hale
Paul Hatalsky
George Hazuka
Casmere Z. Helchowski
Michael Horyczny
Theodore L. Jahimiak
Andrew Jakubkovic
John Jaskolowski
Edward H. Jaworski
Chester Jendrejewski

Steward Jordan
Stanley Kabanowski
Louis Kalem
Chester W. Kaput
Stanley Kavaliunas
John S. Kiempisty
Chester Kilanowski
Joseph T. Kliszcz
Aaron Kogan
Ceslaus Kolakowski
Edward J. Kolakowski
Stanley Konieczny Jr.
Chester Kordas
Alexander Korolchuk
Charles Kovaleski
Chester J. Kozierowski
Edward Krainik
Richard J. Kroth
William Krul
Thaddeus Krygiell
Alfred Kuber
Joseph Kucinski
Albert A. Kukorowski
Walter Kumecki
Chester Kurley
Frank T. Kutyla
Thaddeus C. Kwik
Edmund B. Lang
Benedict A. Langowski
Harry Latkowski

Zygmunt S. Lewall
Edward J. Lewandowski
Henry A. Lewandowski
Leonard Lubanski
Frank Lutostanski
Robert R. Lyons
Edward Malinowski
Chester Maliszewski
Walter W. Macioszczyk
Julian Masternak
Chester M. Masztakowski
Arthur May
Casmere Mazur
William W. Melnyk
Ladislaus M. Miekstyn
Joseph Miela
Julius Minkan
John P. Mironuk Jr.
Konstanty F. Mlynski
Thomas Muszkiewicz Jr.
Zigmunt E. Nadrowski
Walter Niezgocki
Thaddeus Nowak
Bronislaw Nowicki
Edward Olszewski
Walter Opotosky
Wallace Ostrowski
Thaddeus B. Ozinkowski
Patsy Peller
Cass B. Perzanowski
Clarence Pesta
William L Piaseczny
Walter Piechal
Walter Piontkowski
Peter P. Piwonski
Norman Poddam
Roger Pollazzi
Paul Ponican
Barney G. Purtzenski
Harvey Lee Quarrels
Edwin A. Raczkowski
Stanley J. Radzikiewicz
Stephen Rapacki
Gentry E. Reynolds
William Rogowski
Leonard Rostkowski
John J. Rutkowski
Walter Rybicki
Edmund Salata
Dimitro W. Samar
Harry Sawicki
Walter Secosky

Edward L. Serwach
Fred C. Siveck
Leo G. Shiemke
Andy J. Shivak
Joseph J. Sierzan
Sam Simons
Daniel Skikiewicz
Robert E. Skocz
Nicholas Skomas
Stanley Skonieczny
William Slepak
Leonard Smith
Felix Soldenski Jr.
Fred Soloman
Thaddeus J. Sosnowski
John Stachowicz
Walter M. Stolarski
Frank Stroka
Steve Szacum
Casimir W. Szczawinski
Stephen Szczepanski
Carl Szczuka
Arthur W. Szczypek
Walter Szeliga
Leonard J. Szwed
John R. Szymanski
John Targosz
Lucian R. Tarnowski
Adolph J. Trojanowski
Joseph Turczynski
Harry J. Tycholiz
Walter Urbanik
George T. Washington
John Wasko
Leo Werenski
Zigmund Wasolowski
Arthur A. Widowski
Richard John Wilock
Leonard Wilski
Richard R. Winkler
Joseph S. Wisniewski
Sigmund Wisniewski
Edward J. Witkowski
John Wojcik
Edward H. Wojniak
Chester Wojtylo
Chester Zakrzewski
Frank Zborowski
Victor Zegzutor
John Ziolo
Raymond Zussman

ACROSS AMERICA, PEOPLE ARE DISCOVERING SOMETHING WONDERFUL. *THEIR HERITAGE.*

Arcadia Publishing is the leading local history publisher in the United States. With more than 3,000 titles in print and hundreds of new titles released every year, Arcadia has extensive specialized experience chronicling the history of communities and celebrating America's hidden stories, bringing to life the people, places, and events from the past. To discover the history of other communities across the nation, please visit:

www.arcadiapublishing.com

Customized search tools allow you to find regional history books about the town where you grew up, the cities where your friends and family live, the town where your parents met, or even that retirement spot you've been dreaming about.